Quiet Spaces

FOR

Christmas

30 DAYS OF CHRISTMAS DEVOTIONS

ISBN 978-1-998048-06-9

Table of Contents

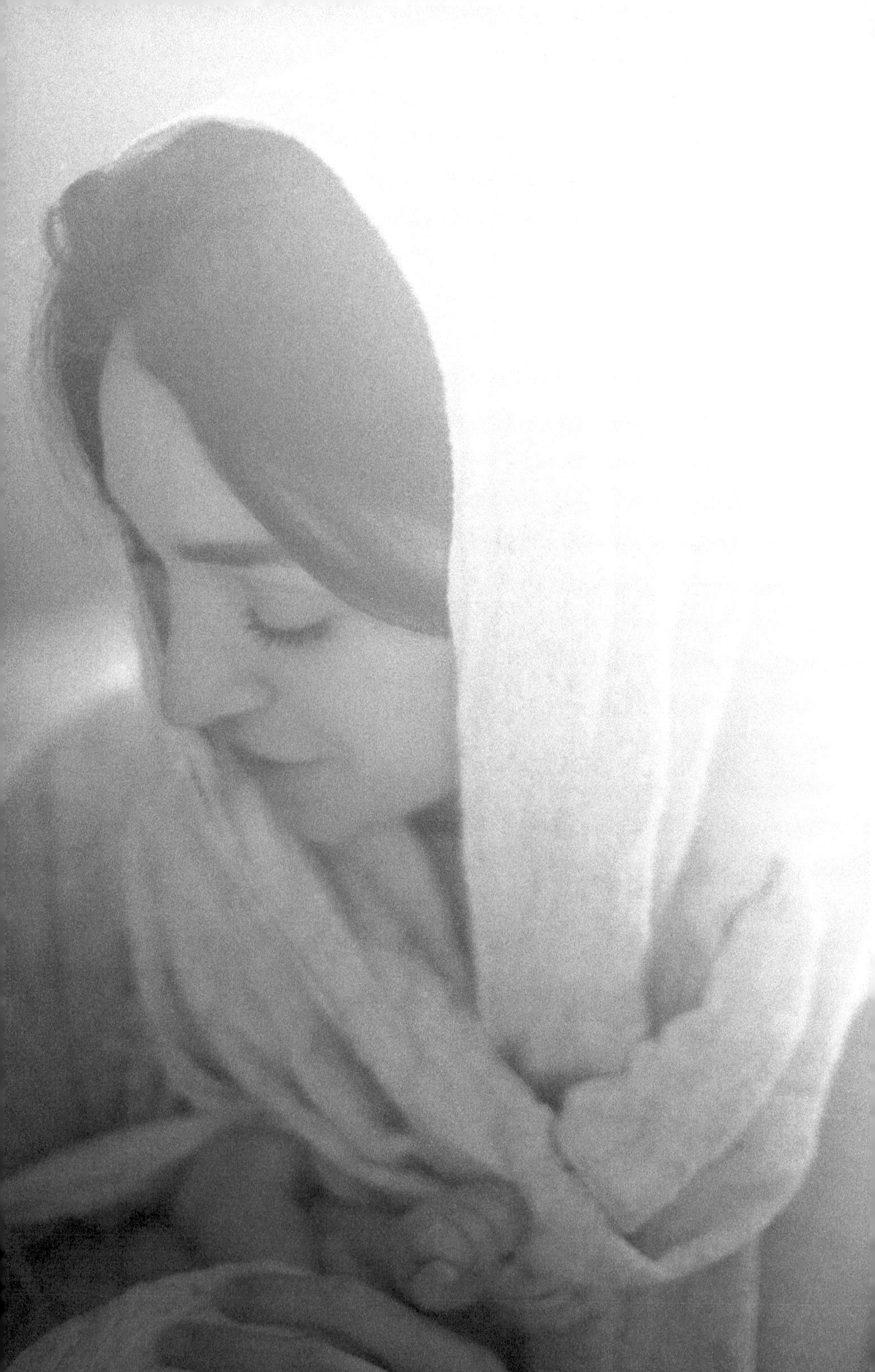

Help Is on the Way!

Advent is the recognition and celebration of the coming of our Lord. It is not simply that He came, but that He still comes to His people. Many assume that Advent and Christmas are the same thing - but you know better. Christmas is the story of Jesus' birth. Advent is the story of waiting. Christmas speaks of an angelic choir, a guiding star, a manger and magi - all part of a specific event. Christ is born! But Advent is about the weeks, months, years and centuries of waiting for Christ to come. Christmas proclaims God is with us. Advent whispers that God is coming. God is always coming to His people.

You are probably busy getting ready for Christmas with shopping, decorating, baking and guestlists. It can be hard to prepare and then be patient for Christmas to arrive, but remember: we are not simply waiting for Christmas – but for Christ.

In this first week, we will reflect on the role and reason for Hope. Using the prophet Isaiah as our guide, we will consider the promises of God and our foundation for hope.

For additional context explore the sermon series, *Christmas in the First Testament,* found on the Back to the Bible Canada website, **backtothebible.ca**

> *"I will not leave you as orphans; I will come to you."*
> *(John 14:18, ESV)*

For many, daily devotionals are not new. You are accustomed to setting time aside daily for God. Still, a brief explanation may be helpful for the start of these next 30 days.

Why Christmas?

There are few seasons of the year that demand more of us. Family obligations and seasonal activity fill our calendar. There is pressure upon our time, thoughts, "to do" list, and pocket book. All of this is done in the name of Jesus. Christmas is about Jesus. Christmas is for Jesus; but if we end our Christmas celebration feeling frazzled, or even distant from Him, have we done it well?

Quiet Spaces for Christmas is offered as an invitation to keep Jesus central in this season. It is opportunity for your heart to be focused daily on our Lord. But it is intended as more than a check on our hearts. It can be a gesture of love for God. Being with Jesus speaks volumes of our devotion for Jesus.

Practical Matters

Each day begins with an opportunity to *"Collect Yourself Before God."* You will find a brief verse from God's prayer book, the Psalms. Read it and allow this moment to be a time for gathering your mind, heart and soul before Him. Frankly, we live scattered lives, piecing ourselves out to the demands of our day. Even in our devotional moments we rush in, cluttered with debris of yesterday and expectations of tomorrow. Allow the Psalm to remind you of God's goodness and presence. Ask God to help you be completely present and attentive to His voice.

You will also find *"God's Promise for Today."* This verse will set the direction for the meditation to follow. Read the verse, but remember this is not simply "table of contents" data. This is God's promise to all of us.

Receive it as such. Consider how this Word from God has a place to land in your life and soul.

After a brief discussion of the Bible text, you will find an invitation to *"Receive God's Promise."* There may be an obvious application for you. There are probably layers of truth that take time to sink in. Do not rush. Hold on to His promise throughout the day.

The time closes with an opportunity to *"Reflect With God."* You may be tempted to see this time as secondary to the reading. Resist that. Prayer is not a postscript. It is the essential focus of our devotion. Give God your heart and allow Him to give you His.

What Are Your Hopes?

We light candles or use special calendars to count down the days to Christmas. Advent is more than a time of waiting - it is a time of watching. We are looking to the coming of Jesus. He came to Bethlehem, but He comes to us daily by His Spirit. He is never far, "in him we live and move and have our being" (Acts 17:28). On this first day, write down your expectations.

- What do you want to receive from God in the next 4 weeks?

- What do you want to offer God through these days?

- Where do you recognize the presence of Jesus for you?

Reflect With God

Open your heart to God in prayer.

Collect Yourself Before God

"Our soul waits for the Lord; he is our help and our shield. For our heart is glad in him, because we trust in his holy name. Let your steadfast love, O Lord, be upon us, even as we hope in you." (Psalm 33:20-22)

God's Promise for Today - *Isaiah 9:2*

"The people who walked in darkness have seen a great light; those who dwelt in a land of deep darkness, on them has light shone."

Consider Today's Truth

Light Is Seen Best in the Dark
G.K. Chesterton wrote in *The Everlasting Man*, "Hope means hoping when things are hopeless, or it is no virtue at all...it is only when everything is hopeless that hope begins to be a strength." In other words, when life seems good, hope may be an idea or casual notion. But when your life is tattered and all support fails, hope becomes a bedrock for perseverance. Hope shines brightest when it is dark.

Isaiah was a prophet from God to Israel in their dark days. For years, the nation had wandered into their own ways and been deaf to the warnings of God. Isaiah preached the coming judgement of God. Yet it was judgement that held mercy. The prophet offered hope for the people. The hope was not rooted in military might, international alliances nor the people's own attempts at reform. God would send the Messiah as both Redeemer and Ruler. He would enlighten us with grace and truth.

God's future promises are as certain as yesterday's news.

Christmas is not the beginning of a promise, but a fulfillment of Messianic predictions made for generations. What was hinted in the very beginning (Genesis 3:15) becomes focused in Isaiah.

The Messiah is God's light amid the darkness (Isaiah 9:2). The hope of His coming illuminated the hearts and minds of God's people. Isaiah wrote in the past tense of the coming future; so certain of God's promise, that it was already considered done! Like a beacon on a shoreline or a beam through a night forest, the light of the Messiah promised rescue, redemption and restoration. When the darkness was thickest, God pierced it with hope. Help was on the way!

"The light shines in the darkness..." (John 1:5)

John tells us that help has come. He points us to Jesus as the light from God who bestows life (John 1:4-18). Jesus is the brilliance of truth and grace. He is the truth from God, revealing the truth about God. He is filled with God's grace, bestowing gift after gift. For those who believe in His Name, He grants the greatest gift of all – to become children of God!

Receive God's Promise

We all struggle - it may be something we're afraid of, worried about, or overcome by. It may be money, health, family tensions, unemployment, loneliness, or depression. It need not be a result of our own actions or missteps; life has a way of falling on us. Regardless, there is reason to hope. The whole Bible tells the same story. God comes to us in our need and rescues us in mercy. Our hope doesn't stand on what we can do, but on what God has done – what God will do. You can turn to Him. You can trust in His grace and power.

Reflect With God

Consider the truth of Isaiah 9:2, and respond to this teaching with prayer.

Collect Yourself Before God

"The Lord is my chosen portion and my cup; you hold my lot. The lines have fallen for me in pleasant places; indeed, I have a beautiful inheritance." (Psalm 16:5-6)

God's Promise for Today - Isaiah 9:6

"For to us a child is born, to us a son is given; and the government shall be upon his shoulder, and his name shall be called Wonderful Counsellor, Mighty God, Everlasting Father, Prince of Peace."

Consider Today's Truth

Charlie or Chase?

When a couple receives news of a pregnancy, they begin a quest to find the right name. It may take nine months to debate, delete and decide. Often a name is chosen to honour family connections. It will become a signature for life, so the name should also carry significant meaning. Parents want the name to "fit" the child's personality and character, but since it's a life yet to be lived, the name is bestowed by hope.

Isaiah promised that those who walk in darkness will see a great light. Like dawn after a stormy night, hope was on the horizon and help was on the way. Just a few verses later, the prophet gives this hope a name, and he uses more than one! These are names which describe family connections, carry eternal significance, and fit the life lived. They are names which convey hope.

Not Just Born, but Sent

Isaiah writes of a "child born" but refines that to "a son is given." This person does not simply arrive, but is sent. It is a Messianic promise. The Messiah will come from God with a mission. Throughout history, many posers and imposters claim to be God's agent. Isaiah reveals the names of the Messiah, that we might be able to identify Him.

The Messiah has a name filled with wonder. He will astonish and amaze. He will be known for the wisdom and truth of His counsel. His power will be greater than men, like that of God's. Time will be in His hands, from the beginning to the end. He will be the means and monarch of peace. Who could fulfill all these names?

The Name Above All Names

These names can be reduced to one: Jesus. Jesus is the child born and the son given. He filled the crowds of His day with wonder, "Can this be the Son of David?" (Matthew 12:23). His disciples marked His wisdom as the "words of life" (John 6:68). His miraculous power was attributed as God's (John 3:2). He is the "Alpha and Omega," the beginning and end of time (Revelation 1:8). He alone is the means of internal peace and peace with God (Romans 5:1). No wonder His name is above all names, worthy of the bended knee and loving praise (Philippians 2:10).

Receive God's Promise

A name does more than identify. A name is something we call upon. We use someone's name when we want or need their presence or help. Of the names predicted by Isaiah, which one do you need today? You may feel bound to this earth, flooded with the mundane – if so, call upon the name of Wonder. If you need wisdom amid confusion, pray to the Counsellor. In weakness, you can ask for the Mighty God. With the chances and changes of life, look to the Everlasting God. In pain, strife or turbulence, there is a Prince of Peace. All these names are doorways to the grace of our God. Know this, when you call upon the name of Jesus, you receive them all.

Reflect With God

Consider the truth of Isaiah 9:6, and respond to this teaching with prayer.

A Baby Makes a Difference

Collect Yourself Before God

"But he would feed you with the finest of the wheat, and with honey from the rock I would satisfy you." (Psalm 81:16)

God's Promise for Today - *Isaiah 9:7*

"Of the increase of his government and of peace there will be no end, on the throne of David and over his kingdom, to establish it and to uphold it with justice and with righteousness from this time forth and forevermore. The zeal of the Lord of hosts will do this."

Consider Today's Truth

Everything Is Different

Parents recall the impact of bringing their first-born child home. They try to prepare themselves, but no one is truly ready for the coming chaos. Sleep schedule, physical fatigue, noise decibels, spousal relationships, the luxury of alone time and the levels of worry and fear - all jolted by the arrival of a child. Who knew that a child could change so much? Isaiah did.

The Messiah Will Reign

Isaiah has already described the coming Messiah with words of hope - wonderful, counsellor, mighty, divine, everlasting and peace. These speak of who the Messiah is, but what will He do? The Messiah will have the responsibility of global rule upon His shoulders. That is His right, as a descendant of David. God keeps His promise to David to set one of his offspring upon his throne (2 Samuel 7:16). His rule will not end despite time or challenges. The rule of the Messiah will increase beyond the borders of Israel into a global Kingdom. His reign will be marked by doing what is right and establishing justice for all. The Prince of Peace will establish peace within His Kingdom. No outside threats, no internal dangers. No strife or protest. Everyone will experience endless Shalom. Should that sound like a fanciful wish, know this: the determination of the Lord is set. He is committed to this promise. He is zealous to do this!

> *"...the Lord Will Give to him the Throne of His father David."*
> *Luke 1:32*

Not only does Jesus fulfill the qualities of the promised Messiah, but He alone is qualified to accomplish the task of the Messiah. Jesus is the Son of David (Matthew 1:1). The Father has given to Jesus the right to judge (John 5:22). Jesus grants peace to replace the world's chaos (John 14:27). He has ascended to the right hand of God and holds all things together by His powerful Word (Hebrews 1:3-4). He will return to earth with His rightful name upon His side, "King of Kings and Lord of Lords" (Revelation 19:16). Isaiah speaks of a son who is given, and He is the rightful king for an everlasting Kingdom.

Receive God's Promise

Christmas is the hope of change - a better change than what politics, education, science, or economics can offer. Our hope doesn't depend upon the best efforts and intentions of humanity. Our hope looks to the son given to us. Jesus alone has the grace, power, credibility, and purity to make this world new. Order will replace chaos. Justice will eliminate self-interest and corruption. All will dwell with safety, security, and peace in the Kingdom of God. And His Kingdom will never end.

Today, as you look around your world, your heart longs for the fullness of His Kingdom. There is much that needs change, so much that you might question the effectiveness of His rule. Take heart. Jesus is Lord today, and while the promises of Isaiah are yet to unfold, we live in hope of "Thy Kingdom come, and Thy will be done." The King has come. The King is coming.

Reflect With God

Consider the truth of Isaiah 9:7, and respond to this teaching with prayer.

Always With Us

Collect Yourself Before God

"Blessed is the man who walks not in the counsel of the wicked, nor stands in the way of sinners, nor sits in the seat of scoffers; but his delight is in the law of the Lord, and on his law he meditates day and night." (Psalm 1:1-2)

God's Promise for Today - Isaiah 7:14

"Therefore the Lord himself will give you a sign. Behold, the virgin shall conceive and bear a son, and shall call his name Immanuel."

Consider Today's Truth

They Come and Go

Our children come and they go. Their arrival transforms the house and the lives of parents. There is a season of firsts, and then a time of independence. But there usually comes a season of leaving - going to college, getting married, moving to another town. The initial home turbulence turns into silence.

What if the child could always be with us? Not as a stunted, immature relationship, but present to us in love, joy, and blessing - always! Isaiah offers such a promise.

If we are to understand Christmas at all, we should do what the New Testament writers did, we should go to Isaiah.

Isaiah and Ahaz

Isaiah's name means, "The Lord saves." That is exactly what Israel needed. Imminent defeat pounded at the city gates. King Ahaz was not a godly man, and he was shaken by the danger. Isaiah carried to the king God's promise of deliverance. Israel's enemies would not succeed. King Ahaz struggled to believe it, so Isaiah told him to ask for a sign from God. The king refused; not because there was nothing that God could do to convince him. The mercy of

God persisted. Isaiah promised a sign from God, not just for the king, but for the whole house of David. It would be a demonstration of the impossible. It would be a sign for life and salvation.

A Virgin Gives Birth

Isaiah promised that a virgin would conceive and give birth to a son. Prophetic words often have two levels of understanding: a near context and a distant one. The near context for King Ahaz was God's assurance of deliverance from enemies. It came true: Jerusalem was not overcome. The distant context is for all of us. The sign from God was the virgin birth of our Saviour. We can be delivered from our sins.

Gabriel promised Mary that the Holy Spirt would conceive within her a child, called the Holy Son of God (Luke 1:35). Those who argue that such a thing is impossible, miss the point. "Nothing is impossible for God!" (Luke 1:37). It takes an impossible sign to demonstrate that this is from God. An impossible birth calls for faith, the very quality King Ahaz lacked. The virgin birth is God's doing. It promises us life - but even more.

Immanuel

The prediction of Isaiah included the name of the child born, Immanuel. Immanuel means, "God with us." There is more than a miracle in the virgin birth. There is the assurance that God is present. God comes to us, where we are, as we are. If God is with us, we are with God.

Receive God's Promise

Jesus is the Son of God who never leaves us. Whether we are alone or in a crowd, He is with us. Your soul is not an empty nest, He is with you, in you. How do you need the presence of God today? How will you welcome the nearness of our Lord? Have hope, He remains Immanuel.

Reflect With God

Consider the truth of Isaiah 7:14, and respond to this teaching with prayer.

Week 1: Hope
When Hope Fades

"Give attention to the sound of my cry, my King and my God, for to you do I pray. O Lord, in the morning you hear my voice; in the morning I prepare a sacrifice for you and watch." (Psalm 5:2-3)

God's Promise for Today - *Isaiah 53:6-7*

"All we like sheep have gone astray; we have turned - every one - to his own way; and the Lord has laid on him the iniquity of us all. He was oppressed, and he was afflicted, yet he opened not his mouth; like a lamb that is led to the slaughter, and like a sheep that before its shearers is silent, so he opened not his mouth."

Consider Today's Truth

The Candle Flickers

If you have watched a burning candle, you know it is susceptible to surrounding conditions. A breeze from an open window. A bump to the table it's on. The length of time it's been burning. All these can cause it to flicker, or even go out. So, it's misleading when the image of a candle in the dark is a metaphor for hope. Hope is not like the candle.

The emotions of hope may vary from excited goosebumps to a tight chest concern. The bumps and breezes of life can cause our hopeful feeling to flicker and fade. But hope is not about our emotional state. It is a decision we make to trust the past and present promises of God. Hope is faith in the future tense. It is a choice towards confidence, even if our surroundings suggest confidence is unfounded.

A Lamb for the Sheep

As Isaiah writes of the coming Messiah, he describes Him as God's servant (Isaiah 52:13). The prophet then describes what will happen to God's Messiah. He begins chapter 53 with an astonished, "Who would believe this?" The Messiah will be ignored, undesired, and the object of scorn. He will even be beaten, wounded, and crushed. Israel's hopes for the coming Messiah did not include ridicule and death. The Messiah was to be victorious and glorious! Instead, the Messiah comes for His flock as a lamb, slaughtered in silence.

Glory in Excelsis

When the angels announced the birth of Jesus, they went first to shepherds, on night watch for their sheep. The shepherds were told that a Saviour was born. He is the Lamb of God (John 1:29). Jesus would be the sacrifice for sin, who laid down His life for us all. Jesus' crucifixion was too much for the Messianic expectations of many. His death caused their hope to flicker. Even Jesus' followers struggled to understand their hope, considering the tragic events (Luke 24:21). But Isaiah predicted this. The servant Lamb of God would die for His wayward sheep. That's what we all are. The Father has laid upon Jesus the Messiah, the iniquity of us all. Our hope has been fulfilled, but not in a manner most expected.

Receive God's Promise

Those who have walked with Jesus for a while can testify that God doesn't follow our agenda or expectations. He doesn't ignore our need or prayers, but neither is He bound by our assumptions. In hope you have prayed for a family member, but the issues have not improved. With hope you have asked God for help and healing, but the sickness remained. You have stood on a promise of God and looked every morning for its arrival. You are still waiting. In all these ways, and more, hope is hard to hold on to. When God doesn't do what we think He would do, our hope can shift to disappointment, even cynicism. You may think that God's delay is because you are unworthy of His action. You don't think God is too small, but your sins are too large.

Hope isn't tied to our worth. It is not a product of sunny days. Hope is the anticipation that God is who He says He is and will do what He said He would do. Look to the Lamb who was slain for you.

Reflect With God

Consider the truth of Isaiah 53:6-7, and respond to this teaching with prayer.

Collect Yourself Before God

"And those who know your name put their trust in you, for you, O Lord, have not forsaken those who seek you." (Psalm 9:10)

God's Promise for Today - *Isaiah 65:17-18*

"For behold, I create new heavens and a new earth, and the former things shall not be remembered or come into mind. But be glad and rejoice forever in that which I create..."

Consider Today's Truth

The Day After

We look forward to Christmas. Year after year, we count down the days, decorate our homes, write both a shopping list and a wish list. We long to be with family and friends to celebrate traditions long held. And year after year, Christmas comes and then it goes. The crescendo leading up to Christmas becomes leftovers, torn wrapping paper, returned gifts and a photo album. It may take a few days, but eventually everything goes back to normal. So, does Christmas really change anything?

Near and Far

Of course, Christmas makes an impact, and one that can be seen up close. The near effects of Bethlehem are witnessed in your own soul.

Jesus has come to save us, and you have tasted His grace. You have believed that the child came to die as a man and now lives as our exalted Lord. Would your life be different if Jesus did not come? The impact of Christmas and Calvary are incalculable to our souls and society. The near effects are seen, celebrated, and proclaimed. But there are far effects that are yet to be.

Over the Horizon of Time

The distance to the horizon at sea level is 4.8 km. That is as far as you can see with the naked eye, and standing still, that is as far as you will ever see. There's a limit to what we can see on earth and in time. Isaiah offers an elevated perspective. He speaks of the changes the Messiah will make beyond the horizon of time. What changes? Everything.

God will change everything. The coming of Jesus and the victory of the cross and empty tomb are the means of God reconciling everything to Himself (Colossians 1:20). The promise of Calvary is that God is making everything new! (Revelation 21:5). A new heaven and a new earth. A time and place where tears are no more, death is non-existent, work is fruitful. Every relationship is love fulfilled and existence is secured with peace and joy. The crooked is straightened. The wrong is made right. The wolf and the lamb will graze together. Nothing will threaten, hurt, or destroy in the dwelling of God. Rather, it will be a place of unwavering gladness and unending worship.

Receive God's Promise

Hope has a near and far context. Many of our hopes are close. New job. Healthy family. Conflicts resolved. Progress of soul. These are petitions and hopes that can be witnessed and celebrated. Of course, not every near hope is fulfilled (remember the candle). Whatever hill or valley we cross in our spiritual walk, we are heading to a certain future. All will be made right and well. While that promise may seem far, nothing will delay or deny the purpose of God to glorify His Name and delight His children with infinite grace spread over unending time. It will be Christmas unending.

Reflect With God

Consider the truth of Isaiah 65:17-18, and respond to this teaching with prayer.

Peace

Rest for Our Souls

Last week, the focus was on Hope - the confident expectation that good was coming from God. Isaiah pointed to the Messiah as God's promise, "Help is on the way!" Of course, looking ahead to better times doesn't relieve the struggle of today. The weeks of Advent turn to Peace - peace in our now. This week we focus in on the experience of Zechariah and Elizabeth. Luke begins his account of Christmas with this elderly couple.

How should we begin the Christmas story? It is a story against all odds. It is a story that can only be explained by a miracle.

If you want to go deeper explore the series entitled, *A Well Researched Christmas*, found on the Back to the Bible Canada website, **backtothebible.ca**

Heard but Unanswered

"My God, my God, why have you forsaken me? Why are you so far from saving me, from the words of my groaning? O my God, I cry by day, but you do not answer, and by night, but I find no rest." (Psalm 22:1-2)

God's Promise for Today - Luke 1:13

"But the angel said to him, 'Do not be afraid, Zechariah, for your prayer has been heard'..."

Consider Today's Truth

"It's too late!"

Those are not good words. When filing taxes, catching a plane, looking for work or buying a house, we don't want to hear, "It's too late." It means the door of opportunity is shut. What we wanted has passed us by. When there is no recourse left, it upsets us, and especially so if we have been talking to God about it. There are occasions when we have prayed about a matter and then, it seems too late.

Looking at What Might Have Been

Zechariah and Elizabeth knew how that felt. These seniors had lived faithful to the Law and were devoted to God. Yet, they were childless. God withheld from them the blessing bestowed upon others. It was a mark of dishonour, if not shame, that they had no son or daughter. Still, their persistent prayers for a child went unanswered. God seemed to be deaf to their pleas. Now, the opportunity for pregnancy was past. They were barren and advanced in years.

Praying When it Makes Little Sense

This married couple remained faithful. There is no hint of bitterness from them in Luke's account. Zechariah served his priestly function, and it seems that they continued to pray when prayer seemed foolish. As Zechariah burned incense within the Temple, Gabriel appeared and shocked Zechariah to the ground. The angel's first words were, "Do not be afraid, for your prayer has been heard!" The angel assures Zechariah that God has been listening to them. God heard their prayer the very first time. He heard it every time that they had asked for a child. God especially heard the prayers that ascended long after anyone thought they would make a difference. God didn't conclude that it was too late. Gabriel promised Zechariah that he and Elizabeth would have a son. To a senior couple whose lives had much more in the past than the future, the angel said, "You will have joy and gladness" (Luke 1:14).

Peace of Being Heard

Zechariah and Elizabeth must have had sleepless nights over the decades. For years they prayed, but nothing happened. It's safe to assume that there were days of despair. We are not told how they held on, but the first angelic words to them were enlightening. God heard them. The confusion of unanswered prayer is often rooted in the questions, "Did God hear me? Is He listening to me? Does He care?" The peaceful resolve to our confusion in prayer is this, "God hears me."

It's true among us. Children, spouses, friends, even enemies, all want to know that they have been heard. When we pray, whatever result comes from our prayers, it begins with being heard. We can find peace knowing that God sees, knows, and hears.

Receive God's Promise

You have something that you have been praying for repeatedly, but it has not yet happened. What is it? What are your feelings about God's denial or delay? It can be confusing, painful, or even faith shaking. Let Gabriel's assurance become your comfort, "Your prayer has been heard!" Peace of soul arrives through different paths, but it begins by knowing that God is not insensitive to your cries. Bethlehem is proof that the prayers of God's people have been heard. He has given us His Son. He has given Himself.

Reflect With God

Consider the truth of Luke 1:13, and respond to this teaching with prayer.

Collect Yourself Before God

"I call upon you, for you will answer me, O God; incline your ear to me; hear my words. Wondrously show your steadfast love, O Savior of those who seek refuge from their adversaries at your right hand." (Psalm 17:6-7)

God's Promise for Today - *Luke 1:22*

"And when he came out, he was unable to speak to them, and they realized that he had seen a vision in the temple. And he kept making signs to them and remained mute."

Consider Today's Truth

Lost for Words

What's the longest you have ever gone without speaking? Whether it was a medical issue or a personal choice in a time of solitude, you know, being silent is hard! Daily, we use our voice to communicate needs, instructions, intensions, opinions, and feelings. If required, we can communicate by other means, but speaking is personal. We are known by our voice. When we can't speak, we mute part of ourselves.

Struck Dumb

Gabriel was sent to give good news to Zechariah. The very thing he and Elizabeth prayed for would happen; they would have a child! If he had received this angelic visit years ago, Zechariah's reaction may have been different. But he and Elizabeth were past the years of pregnancy. Zechariah challenged Gabriel's message with the fact of their age. The problem was, Zechariah wasn't considering all the facts. He ignored the fact of an angelic visitation from the one who "stands in the presence of God." He skipped past the example of Abraham and Sarah. He didn't consider where he was standing, in the Temple where God dwells. All he saw was years of nothing happening and the biological condition that refused to yield to his wishes. He heard the news, but he didn't believe it. In consequence, Gabriel took Zechariah's voice from him. He would not be able to speak until the promise of God was fulfilled.

Can't Bless, Just Shrug

Zechariah had a priestly duty to perform. He entered the Temple to offer incense, symbolic of the prayers of God's people. He was there on their behalf. Once the incense was offered, he was to exit the Temple and pronounce God's blessing upon them. He was to assure them that their prayers were heard and announce the priestly blessing (Numbers 6:24-26). He couldn't do it. He had no voice, and therefore, the people had no pronounced blessing.

You can imagine the confusion. The crowd knew something happened, but Zechariah was unable to do what was needed. Obviously, Zechariah had other means of communication. He probably wrote the details of Gabriel's message when he got home to Elizabeth. But what matters in the text is this; the blessing that should have been declared upon the people, wasn't. Why? Because doubt has nothing to say.

Christmas is a time in which the old story is just too difficult for some to believe.

Doubt Is a Gag

When we don't believe the good news that God is granting us, we too have nothing to say. We are stifled from praise, gratitude, or blessing.

We have nothing encouraging or promising to voice to our family, friends, or co-workers. What could be shared as hope in God's promises is muffled because we don't believe them ourselves. Doubt is more than silence. It is an obstacle to peace.

Receive God's Promise

Faith is the means of our salvation. It is also the root and reason for sharing good news from God. We are reminded that whatever good we have to say in this world springs out of faith. "I believed and so I speak"(2 Corinthians 4:13). Everyone's faith has vulnerabilities, room to grow. "Lord, I believe, help my unbelief!" (Mark 9:25). Where do you want God to increase your faith? In His power, faithfulness, wisdom, mercy, grace, or justice? As our faith convictions grow in God, we have good news to proclaim about God.

Reflect With God

Consider the truth of Luke 1:22, and respond to this teaching with prayer.

Setting God's Table

Collect Yourself Before God

"The LORD is my rock and my fortress and my deliverer, my God, my rock, in whom I take refuge, my shield, and the horn of my salvation, my stronghold. I call upon the LORD, who is worthy to be praised, and I am saved from my enemies." (Psalm 18:2-3)

God's Promise for Today - *Luke 1:17*

"And he will go before him in the spirit and power of Elijah, to turn the hearts of the fathers to the children, and the disobedient to the wisdom of the just, to make ready for the Lord a people prepared."

Consider Today's Truth

People Get Ready

Most things in life require preparation. Meals don't just happen. Retirement requires years of investment. A nursery is prepped early for the baby. We study for tests and plan our weddings. The degree of our preparation often says something about the importance of an event. It also says something about us. "Winging it" is not always a helpful philosophy for life. We need to be equipped and ready for the things that matter.

Trailblazer

Before God sent His Son to earth, He sent a forerunner. Gabriel told Zechariah to name his future son "John" - later known as "John the Baptist." This boy would flood the heart of his parents with joy, and this joy would be shared by many. John would be great in the eyes of God and man. He would fulfill the calling of a Nazarite, one who is dedicated wholly to God. He would be the instrument of God's Spirit, even from the womb. John would reflect the ministry and voice of Elijah the prophet. This boy would be God's invitation to the Christ and turn the spotlight on Jesus. But even before that, there was preparatory work to do. John was to ensure that the people were ready for Jesus. How?

Turn Around!

The ministry of John the Baptist would be a call to repentance. He wore the attire of a prophet and lived in isolation from society. But the crowds came to him, compelled by his message. John warned that they couldn't rely on their Abrahamic ancestry to save them. He cautioned of greed and hypocrisy. He called for heart changes that would be evidenced by water baptism. He spoke of a fire coming that would purge the people, and that God would sweep the nation like a man cleans out his barn (Luke 3:1-17). John was raising the nation's consciousness of sin and their need for forgiveness. He was getting the nation ready for Jesus, the Lamb of God.

Honey or Vinegar?

We don't hear much about repentance in church these days. The mindset seems to be that we will attract people to God if we are more accommodating and approachable. More honey, less vinegar. That was not the way of John the Baptist. If the people were to understand the message and means of grace through Jesus, they would have to recognize the holiness of God and the ways they fell short of it. It is no different today.

Repentance remains a necessary message. There is no call to be abusive or cruel, but the need for heart change and our inability to do it ourselves is part of the good news we proclaim. Unless people understand their need for Jesus, the good news is just news. It becomes good when we realize that our sins are many, that righteousness is beyond us and that God has made a way by faith in Jesus Christ.

Receive God's Promise

Christmas can be nothing more than sentiment. Warm feelings, family gatherings, traditional songs, peaceful wishes. But Christmas is much more. It speaks of God coming to us in our helplessness. He comes to rescue us. He comes with grace for our sins. Take away the message of our sins, and Christmas is reduced to wintery festivals and sleigh rides. You can be a forerunner for Jesus today. Being both gracious and truthful, you can point to the Saviour. You can speak the good news that Jesus is the means of the forgiveness we need and the peace we pray for.

Reflect With God

Consider the truth of Luke 1:17, and respond to this teaching with prayer.

Week 2: Peace
Something to Talk About

Collect Yourself Before God

"The Lord looks down from heaven on the children of man, to see if there are any who understand, who seek after God." (Psalm 14:2)

God's Promise for Today - Luke 1:65-66

"And fear came on all their neighbors. And all these things were talked about through all the hill country of Judea, and all who heard them laid them up in their hearts, saying, 'What then will this child be?' For the hand of the Lord was with him."

Consider Today's Truth

A Public Declaration

These days it is common to have a gender reveal party. Parents gather family and friends to reveal whether their coming child is a boy or a girl. They may loft blue balloons for a boy, or release pink smoke for a girl. Whatever creative means they use, it is meant for joyful celebration.

In similar fashion, Zechariah and Elizabeth gathered family and townspeople for a declaration about their child, not the gender, but his name. Their son was to be circumcised eight days after birth, and it was unusual that he hadn't yet been named. Relatives didn't think that his name was much of an issue. He would be named after his father of course! The fact that Elizabeth conceived was a wonder, and it seemed obvious that they would not have any more children. Certainly the child would be called Zechariah.

Loosed Lips

Elizabeth was clear, the boy would be called "John." Zechariah had informed Elizabeth what Gabriel had told him. Both parents wanted to obey God and thus honour Him for His gift of a son. Relatives argued with Elizabeth and looked for a final decision from Zechariah. For 9 months he hadn't said a word. Since he couldn't speak, he asked for a tablet and wrote, "His name is John!" The confusion of the relatives shifted into astonishment. As soon as Zechariah wrote those words, his speech returned. He spoke the praises of God for all He had done. At first Zechariah doubted, but Elizabeth conceived just as Gabriel said. His disbelief became faith and in a moment of obedience, his faith became praise.

A Portent of Promise

During the family celebration and Zechariah's loud, probably unstoppable voice, something shifted. Among the townspeople, joy morphed to wonder, and wonder settled deeper as fear. It wasn't a fear of dread, but a sense of awe. Something large was happening. Zechariah claimed to be visited by an angel from God and was mute as a result. The elderly couple conceived when it was impossible to do so. The name of the child born broke family and town tradition. Now Zechariah was using every word he had saved for nine months to praise God. The town recognized that God's Hand was in all of this. They gossiped about the details until the hill country of Judea was filled with the story. The marketplace echoed it. People reflected on the reported events and wondered, "What is God doing? What will this child be?" God was with the child John. What did it mean?

Receive God's Promise

We can't do what God does. God's will and work belong only to Him. But we can participate in His work in two fundamental necessities. We can trust and obey. That's the message from Zechariah. The promises of God are sure, and we are called to believe. When our faith is translated into obedience, our family, friends, neighbours and strangers will marvel at what God is doing. Our faith and obedience become invitation for others to consider the ways and will of God. Let your life be a proclamation that God is at work. He will receive just praise from many.

Reflect With God

Consider the truth of Luke 1:65-66, and respond to this teaching with prayer.

Collect Yourself Before God

"To you, O Lord, I lift up my soul. O my God, in you I trust; let me not be put to shame; let not my enemies exult over me." (Psalm 25:1-2)

God's Promise for Today - *Luke 1:68-70*

"Blessed be the Lord God of Israel, for he has visited and redeemed his people and has raised up a horn of salvation for us in the house of his servant David, as he spoke by the mouth of his holy prophets from of old."

Consider Today's Truth

It Sticks Us Together

Trust is the glue in all our relationships. Wedding vows are made, and it's trust in those vows that empowers perseverance. Friends trust one another with their secrets. Employers and employees put trust in mutual obligations. Cynicism about politics is stoked by broken trust. In every relationship we have, trust is a necessary ingredient. So, it shouldn't surprise us that trust is the quality that God smiles at in our relationship with Him. Without faith, it is impossible to please Him (Hebrews 11:6).

Worthy of Trust

Once Zechariah began to speak, his words were like a song in two verses. The second verse (Luke 1:76-79) was addressed to his son John. The primary verse (Luke 1:68-75) was a declaration of praise with one central truth. "God has kept His promise!" The Old Testament is a promise. From Genesis to Malachi, God had pledged to send a Redeemer. This Messiah would bruise the head of the serpent (Genesis 3:15), sit on David's Throne (2 Samuel 7:12-13) and fulfill the covenant of God (Malachi 3:1-4). Zechariah proclaims that God has now fulfilled His pledge. Jesus the Messiah has come.

God has proved Himself worthy of trust. He has done for us what He said He would do. Our trust in God is not rooted in His power or wisdom. We do not trust Him because He is infinite and timeless. God is all of this in perfection and more; but we trust Him because He is faithful to His Word. An almighty god who didn't keep his promise would not be trusted. A being with unmatched wisdom but fickle ways can't be depended upon. But our God is perfectly unfailing. He can be trusted to do what He said He would do.

Delivered to Serve

Our trust in God leads to unfettered service for Him. Because God can be trusted, we can serve Him without fear. That is the declaration of Zechariah (Luke 1:74-75). We are delivered by God's grace and freed to give our complete lives to Him. We need not fear the threats around us nor doubt the certain victory in front of us. We can serve Him wholly because He can be trusted wholly. During hardship, challenges or personal weakness, our souls can be comforted by this. God is faithful. Peace is possible.

Receive God's Promise

It may help to take some quiet moments and consider the areas where you find it hard to trust God. Don't be ashamed to admit it, in fact, unless we look at those areas honestly, we will never change. Is it in matters of health, finances, relationships, security or forgiveness? Consider the place of struggle and begin to read afresh the promises of God about that issue. What does God say? Has God been faithful in the past? Can He be trusted for the future? Ask God to undergird this vulnerability with His grace and peace.

Reflect With God

Consider the truth of Luke 1:68-70, and respond to this teaching with prayer.

Week 2: Peace
Peace Here and Now

Collect Yourself Before God

"One thing have I asked of the Lord, that will I seek after: that I may dwell in the house of the Lord all the days of my life, to gaze upon the beauty of the Lord and to inquire in his temple." (Psalm 27:4)

God's Promise for Today - *Luke 1:78-79*

"Because of the tender mercy of our God whereby the sunrise shall visit us from on high to give light to those who sit in darkness and in the shadow of death, to guide our feet into the way of peace."

Consider Today's Truth

Peace on Earth?

You hear it every year. On Christmas cards, from Sunday School angels, and carols of the season, "Peace on earth." And every year it seems like a wish and not a reality. Henry Longfellow wrote a poem, eventually put to music, "I Heard the Bells on Christmas Day." In the first verse, the bells chime the promise of peace. But with stark honesty, the following verse says, "'There is no peace on earth.' I said, 'For hate is strong, and mocks the song of peace of earth, good will to men.'" Longfellow wrote the poem in 1863, in the years of the American Civil War. Is the world in our day any more peaceful?

The Patient Inevitable Work of God

After Zechariah spoke of God keeping His promises to humanity, he looked at his son and spoke of his future (Luke 1:76-79). John the Baptist would prepare the way for Jesus. His preaching would reveal sin and point to the Lamb of God who takes away sin. In Jesus, there is hope for mercy and light to live by. More so, Jesus will "guide our feet into the way of peace." Peace is a path we walk upon and a destination we walk towards. It takes time.

More Than a Feeling

We tend to think of peace as a tranquil feeling, or perhaps negotiated settlements between nations. It can be both, but clearly it is more. Jesus did not die to grant us serenity or to end war in our time. Peace is a state of reconciliation with God. As we are justified and forgiven, we have peace with God (Romans 5:1). That peace becomes a foundation for reconciliation with one another (Romans 12:8). While our peace with God is instantly imputed by faith, the peace between one another is a path we walk upon. We build peace. It doesn't come ready made. This too is peace made possible through Jesus Christ.

God Is Not Done

While Longfellow despaired because of the absence of "peace on earth" in his day, he understood the pace and direction of God's working. As the bells continued to ring, he wrote,

"God is not dead, nor doth He sleep;
The wrong shall fail,
the right prevail,
With Peace on earth,
good will to men."

The Kingdom of peace is unfolding, day by day, heart by heart. God will end all warfare. He will still every hostility. Until that day, each of us has a path of peace to walk upon.

Receive God's Promise

It's ironic. The promise of peace is heralded in a season when peace can be hard to find. It is a short time until Christmas Day, and it is getting shorter! You may be feeling the tension of a "to do" list that seems to get larger every day. You might sense the weight of financial pressure and the urge to make everybody happy. Family gatherings are not always pleasant and peaceful. You may be facing Christmas alone this year. The scurry and perceived obligations try to rob us of peace. Take time each day to do what matters. Give your heart to God in prayer. Clutch the centrality of the message that God has come to you with grace and truth. Hold on to what counts and release all the rest. Peace.

Reflect With God

Consider the truth of Luke 1:78-79, and respond to this teaching with prayer.

Week 2: Peace
The Spirit of Christmas

Collect Yourself Before God

"Ascribe to the Lord, O heavenly beings, ascribe to the Lord glory and strength." (Psalm 29:1)

God's Promise for Today - Luke 1:80

"And the child grew and became strong in spirit, and he was in the wilderness until the day of his public appearance to Israel."

Consider Today's Truth

It Doesn't Feel Like Christmas

Has Christmas ever arrived, and you didn't feel ready? The shopping is done, and the gifts are wrapped. The menu is planned, and the house is festive. The guestroom is set for visits. You've done everything that needs be done, but you still don't feel ready. "I'm not in the Christmas mood." Christmas carols, sleigh rides, eggnog and family traditions don't seem to work. So how do you get into the spirit of Christmas?

And the Child Grew

The account of Zechariah and Elizabeth ends with a summation statement about the boy John. His developing years were marked by growth. His early adult years were spent in isolation until his public ministry. We may assume certain facets of his early growth, language, height, strength, and social skills. But that is not what Luke mentions. We are told that the boy became strong in spirit. If we assume that Luke is referring to personality and character, we miss a central thrust of this story.

John was filled with the Holy Spirit before he was born (Luke 1:15). He was endued with the Spirit of God even as Elijah was (Luke 1:17). When Luke tells us that John grew strong in the Spirit, it is a statement of God's power within him. As a boy, John learned to listen to the voice of the Spirit, to surrender to the Spirit's leading and to trust the Spirit's power. It was an education that continued in the wilderness and was evidenced in his ministry.

Woven into the Story

Mention of the Spirit of God is repeated in the story of Zechariah and Elizabeth. John was filled with the Spirit in his mother's womb, and leaped within the womb at the sound of Mary's voice (Luke 1:41). Elizabeth was filled with the Spirit and blessed Mary, her relative (Luke 1:41). Zechariah was filled with the Spirit when he prophesied about his son's future ministry (Luke 1:67), It becomes clear that we can't tell the Christmas story without reference to the presence and power of the Holy Spirit. We can't celebrate Christmas without that same presence and power.

We Don't Make Christmas

Christmas is not something we make with our traditions and celebrations. Christmas is God's doing. He sent His Son to earth, conceived by the Spirit. Christmas is His gift to us. And while the centuries have passed, the Spirit today is still pointing to Jesus. The Spirit reveals the truth of His coming and the wonder of the Father's grace. It is the work of the Spirit to grant peace for Christmas and beyond. The mood of Christmas is what society and families have generated. It comes and goes. The Spirit of Christmas is the work of God in and through us.

Receive God's Promise

Like the wrappings of a gift, the traditions of Christmas may be fun to observe, but they can be discarded, and the gift remains. Ask yourself; "Are you trying to make Christmas happen?" or "Are you surrendered to the grace God has for you?" Spend time in prayer, not simply for peace; but to be present and open to what God wants to do by His Spirit in and through you. Let God bring Christmas to you.

Reflect With God

Consider the truth of Luke 1:80, and respond to this teaching with prayer.

He Shall Save His People

It is sung as the "most wonderful time of the year!" To state the obvious, Christmas is a time for joy! It offers excitement, goosebumps, delight, and celebration. The question is not whether Christmas brings joy, but rather, "What is the reason for our joy at Christmas?" This Advent week, we will focus on Joy and the foundation for it. We will highlight Joseph's perspective through Matthew's account.

For more, we encourage you to spend time in the sermon series, *Christmas Unplugged,* found on the Back to the Bible Canada website, **backtothebible.ca**

Collect Yourself Before God

"But I trust in you, O Lord; I say, 'You are my God.' My times are in your hand; rescue me from the hand of my enemies and from my persecutors! Make your face shine on your servant; save me in your steadfast love!" (Psalm 31:14-16)

God's Promise for Today - *Matthew 1:18*

"Now the birth of Jesus Christ took place in this way..."

Consider Today's Truth

Don't Wreck Christmas!

When did you tell your children that there was no Santa Claus? Perhaps you never started the fable, or you let your child grow out of it on their own. Some parents struggle with the dilemma. They foster the story of the "merry elf" early, but then worry that when the children discover the truth, their Christmas will be ruined!

It can be challenging to celebrate Christmas with the blending of family or societal traditions and the biblical account. What do we do with Christmas trees, gift exchanges, seasonal songs, a global ride of reindeer and even the date, December 25th?

None of that is in the Bible account, but in our culture, Christmas is saturated with it.

In the midst of Christmas fairy tales and legends and traditions ...do you see the real story?

Is Matthew a Grouch?

Matthew's account of Jesus' birth doesn't have any of our traditions built in. In fact, Matthew strips Christmas down even further. He doesn't write of shepherds keeping watch at night. He doesn't speak of the angelic choir and refers to Bethlehem only in a passing manner (Matthew 12:1). The manger is not mentioned, and he skips over the birth of Jesus in a, "Oh by the way" manner! (Matthew 1:25). And then Matthew tears at our perception of Christmas with a sword. He speaks of deception, disillusionment, danger, and death. He sings in a minor key and paints with grey and black. This is not the sound and look of the Christmas we expect. Where is the Christmas joy?

Christmas Doesn't Have to Be Pristine

There is no sentiment in Matthew's story of Jesus' birth. In place of warm feelings, there is confusion and fear. Terror replaces tinsel. It forces us to reflect on the way we celebrate the season. We work to ensure that our Christmas is filled with pleasant thoughts. The turkey should be moist and the table conversation congenial. Every child must relish every gift. The tree won't fall over, and every family member arrives home. The joy of Christmas is proportionate to the quality of our celebration. Christmas must be perfect!

Matthew denies that. His account deals with life as it is, not as we want it to be. Matthew shows God coming to the real world, not a Christmas card of glitter. Jesus is born to a place where wicked kings try to kill babies, families must flee for their lives and the Son of God becomes a refugee in a foreign country. Jesus didn't delay His arrival until the world got better. He came to rescue the world in its brokenness. That is a reason for joy.

Receive God's Promise

Matthew's Christmas story begins, "Now the birth of Jesus Christ took place in this way..." He then describes a way that has shadows and doubt. It is an honest story that has the authenticity of our real world. Will you be authentic this Christmas? Can you set aside pretense and just be who you are and where you are? There may be relational struggles. Perhaps there are limited funds available, and your table is sparse. You may be forcing a smile and a song. Know this: Jesus came to meet us exactly as we are. Welcoming Jesus to our "less than ideal state" is exactly the way to celebrate Christmas.

Reflect With God

Consider the truth of Matthew 1:18, and respond to this teaching with prayer.

Collect Yourself Before God

"I will instruct you and teach you in the way you should go; I will counsel you with my eye upon you. Be not like a horse or a mule, without understanding, which must be curbed with bit and bridle, or it will not stay near you." (Psalm 32:8-9)

God's Promise for Today - *Matthew 1:1*

"The book of the genealogy of Jesus Christ, the son of David, the son of Abraham."

Consider Today's Truth

Traced Your Roots?

Today it is relatively easy to trace your relatives. Technology allows us to map our DNA and discover our ancestral line. Perhaps you have done it. You may have found some surprises, or confirmed the generational stories passed down. As interesting as that history is, I am sure not one of us begins Christmas Day with it. We wouldn't think of gathering the family around the tree and before anything else, recite the list of unknown names long passed. Like the opening credits of a movie, we want to skip the data and get to the story! Matthew ignores our impatience and begins the story of Jesus' birth with a list of 42 ancestors, many long forgotten and ignored.

Kings, Prostitutes and Gentiles

So why does Matthew begin his gospel in the most boring manner possible? As one of the 12 disciples of Jesus, he could have started with a dramatic miracle or an interesting quote from Jesus. Instead, the accountant in him begins with a ledger of people whose sum is Jesus. And frankly, some of the names don't seem to add up!

It makes sense to include David and Abraham. That gives Jesus a royal descent and a claim to the father of faith. But Matthew includes some shady and sordid people. Manasseh was the worst king in Israel's history (Matthew 1:10). Rahab was a prostitute and Ruth was a Gentile (Matthew 1:5). These are not the people you highlight in your family credentials! It is a messy list, but a list which ties Jesus to Israel's history and announces Him as the rightful heir to David's throne. Matthew wants us to know that God is a covenant keeper, and Jesus is His King who fulfills the covenant He has made.

God Rules Over All

We can be guilty of making promises we cannot keep, despite our best intentions. Flat tires, bad weather, delayed planes, illness, or unforeseen circumstances can frustrate and deny our promises. We don't have the power or control to promise that we will be any place tomorrow. Yet God can make promises to Abraham and David and shape time and space to ensure that His Word will come true. Consider the centuries God controlled and the geography He spanned to have Jesus born in Bethlehem. Think of the lives He moved, so that the right people met, married, and had children leading to Joseph and Mary. It boggles the mind! God worked through sinful people and less than ideal conditions to ensure the birth of Jesus. God did not hasten, nor did He delay. He was patient and purposeful. While people may have questioned and doubted, nothing would frustrate His power and plans.

Receive God's Promise

And that is why you are here. Clearly, we are not the fulfilment of covenantal promise, but the hand of God is sovereign upon you even as it was upon every name Matthew wrote. You live because God wanted you to live. He placed you in the right country and town. He gave you your family. He rules over your life experience. Your life is not chance. The struggles are part of His plan. You are His workmanship created in Christ Jesus (Ephesians 2:10). This Christmas, consider the following: your life is His gift, just as it is.

Reflect With God

Consider the truth of Matthew 1:1, and respond to this teaching with prayer.

It's Not Supposed to Be Like This

"Return, O my soul, to your rest; for the Lord has dealt bountifully to you."
(Psalm 116:7)

God's Promise for Today - *Matthew 1:18-19*

"...When his mother Mary had been betrothed to Joseph, before they came together she was found to be with child from the Holy Spirit. And her husband Joseph, being a just man and unwilling to put her to shame, resolved to divorce her quietly."

Consider Today's Truth

That's Not What I Wanted

The expectations we bring to Christmas are so inflated, a measure of deflation is inevitable. The sweater was not what we hoped for. The phone call we expected didn't happen. The Christmas bonus was too late and too little. We set ourselves up to be crestfallen, often over minor things. But there are major events that can impact the season.

The first Christmas after the passing of a loved one is a significant hurdle. Maybe a daughter enters rehab in December, or a son is transferred overseas in November. There can be a variety of struggles that make us think, "This isn't the Christmas I expected or wanted." Joseph understands situations like these.

Joseph's Dilemma

Joseph and Mary were betrothed - that is, their families arranged for them to be married. Agreements and promises were made in the presence of witnesses. While they lived in separate homes until their nuptials, this was a legal contract of marriage. Joseph and Mary had to be filled with hopes and plans. Their future was as husband and wife. They would build a home together. Their intentions were almost derailed.

Joseph learned of Mary's pregnancy. We assume that Mary told him of the angelic visit and of the miracle of a virgin birth. Joseph could not wrap his head around Mary's explanation. She was pregnant, and Joseph knew he couldn't be the father. He was torn in two directions. Being a just man, he knew that the marriage could not happen. Mary's supposed unfaithfulness put an end to it. A just man doesn't marry an adulteress. Divorce was possible, but Joseph didn't want to shame Mary with a public process. His recourse was to divorce her quietly. He would end the relationship and spare her humiliation.

We often rush through the story and get to the happy resolve. We shouldn't go so fast. Matthew invites us to consider Joseph's position. He felt betrayed by his future wife and heartbroken with disappointment. He is confused and angry. The first scene Matthew paints for us to present the arrival of Jesus is a painful conversation between two tear-stained faces and the crushing decision to end what could have been. Then Jesus comes.

Receive God's Promise

Matthew reminds us of Isaiah's promise that the Son to be born of a virgin would be called Immanuel - "God is with us" (Matthew 1:23). When our dreams are broken, God is with us. When life doesn't act as we expect, God is with us. When the dearest relationships we have are threatened with loss, God is with us. Whatever pain you are feeling of body or soul, God is with you. Whatever fear or doubt you have, He is near. In the midst of trauma, He is at your side. However you need the presence of Jesus in this season, know that you already have it.

Reflect With God

Consider the truth of Matthew 1:18-19, and respond to this teaching with prayer.

Faith Trusts the Impossible

Collect Yourself Before God

"Your steadfast love, O Lord, extends to the heavens, your faithfulness to the clouds. Your righteousness is like the mountains of God; your judgments are like the great deep; man and beast you save, O Lord." (Psalm 36:5-6)

God's Promise for Today - Matthew 1:24-25

"When Joseph woke from sleep, he did as the angel of the Lord commanded him: he took his wife, but knew her not until she had given birth to a son. And he called his name Jesus."

Consider Today's Truth

I Had a Weird Dream Last Night

You have probably had strange dreams that made no sense in the morning. People from your long ago show up in places they shouldn't be. Your dog talks to you and explains the need for better kibble. You are standing before a crowd to give a speech, totally unprepared and lacking an important item of clothing. What do you make of these dreams? Probably nothing. It's flotsam of the brain and you would never act on it.

An Angel at Night

Dreams are a thread woven throughout Matthew's narrative of Jesus' birth. God warns the Magi in a dream to avoid King Herod (Matthew 1:12). Joseph is commanded by God in a dream to flee into Egypt (Matthew 1:13). He is told to return to Israel in a dream and guided to Galilee in the same manner (Matthew 1:19-22). It was a dream that assured Joseph that he should take Mary as his wife (Matthew 1:20).

The news of Mary's pregnancy was heavy on Joseph's mind. He couldn't understand it and didn't want to divorce her but saw no other option. As he wrestled with his thoughts and feelings at night, God met him in a dream. The Lord affirmed the moral character of Mary and the miracle of her virgin conception. Joseph was told that she would have a son. Joseph was to name Him Jesus. The confusion Joseph felt was relieved that all of this was by the Holy Spirit. God was at work.

Faith of Joseph

After a dream like that, what do you do in the morning? Do you relegate it into the category of other weird dreams you've had? Do you attribute it to your own wishful thinking, justified by a dream? Do you ignore it because you've never had a dream like this before? All these options and more were available to Joseph. He chose none of them. When he awoke, the first thing he did was go to Mary and explain what happened. Now they both had divine visitation accounts, and they meshed into one narrative. Joseph took Mary as his wife, and she would have a son.

Joseph is described as a just man, one who does what is right. He was also a man of faith, one who does as God directs. Joseph chose to believe what God told him. He obeyed God's directive despite town gossip and the critical whispers of dispersion. Joseph trusted an impossible message about a virgin birth, not simply at the word of Mary, but at the Word of God.

Receive God's Promise

God has employed various ways to communicate His Word and Will, but our confidence now rests in Jesus as His full declaration (Hebrews 1:1-2). Dreams are not our authority for faith, Jesus is. Our faith in Jesus and His Word is evidenced by our obedience. We hear, trust and act. That is not always easy. We may have questions and hesitations. The story of Joseph demonstrates that confusion, doubt and fear are resolved by the faith we place in God's Word and the obedience that flows from it.

Reflect With God

Consider the truth of Matthew 1:24-25, and respond to this teaching with prayer.

"Trust in the Lord and do good; dwell in the land and befriend faithfulness. Delight yourself in the Lord, and he will give you the desires of your heart." (Psalm 37:3-4)

God's Promise for Today - Matthew 1:21

"She will bear a son, and you shall call his name Jesus, for he will save his people from their sins."

Consider Today's Truth

Names Matter

Names were often attributed according to your job, location, or physical trait. If your last name is "George", there is a farmer in your background. If your mail is addressed to "Mrs. Berg", someone from your past used to live by a mountain. "Billy Brown" likely came from a gene pool of brown hair. In other words, names are meant to say something about us. They are the means of distinguishing us from those who had blonde hair, lived by a creek, or worked as a blacksmith.

Call Me Joe

Joseph was instructed in a dream to call Mary's son, Jesus. To most of us, the name "Jesus" is so special, that we would hesitate to call our son that today. The name has justly been adorned with honour and devotion. Like the chorus says, "There's just something about that name." Yet in the time of Joseph, the name Jesus was quite common. It was the equivalent of "Joe" today. There were other little boys who had the name Jesus, and we can find several named Jesus in the New Testament.

Jesus is the Greek form of the Jewish name Joshua. Parents were prone to name their son after the Old Testament hero. Joshua was a conqueror who led Israel into the promised land. His name means "Jehovah saves" and that is what God did for His people. The name Jesus means the same - "Jehovah saves." That is what Jesus did for His people. While the name Jesus was common, Mary's son would set Himself apart and fulfill the meaning of His name. Jesus was not unique because of the name He was given, but because He was God's instrument of deliverance for mankind. Joseph was told, "Call Him Jesus for He shall save His people from their sins."

Joy of Being Rescued

Our society treats Christmas as if it was the epitome of celebrations. It feels like a highlight of the year. But believers understand that Bethlehem is the beginning of our salvation. Easter is the fulfillment. We rejoice at Christmas because God has begun redemption. We worship at Easter because God has finished redemption. The joy of Christmas is great. The joy of Easter is greater.

Jesus would grow in wisdom, stature and in favour with God and man (Luke 2:52). He left Joseph's trade of carpentry to fulfill His heavenly Father's will. Jesus began to preach the Kingdom of God, extend miraculous mercy to the blind and lame, and teach the wisdom of God's rule. He gathered 12 learners around Him and deputized them for the spread of the Kingdom. Ultimately, Jesus surrendered Himself as God's sacrifice for the sins of humanity. The sinless lamb died to atone for our broken ways, rebellious hearts, and repeated failures. When all seemed lost and buried in a tomb, Jesus rose in power and glory. His righteousness becomes our goodness. His victory becomes our win. His life is now our life. His name becomes our worship and joy. He saves us from our sin.

Receive God's Promise

If we don't honour Jesus, Christmas is just a party - a festive, costly, onerous season that dissipates in days. If we ignore the reason He came, our celebrations lack meaning. Take time today to thank God for His salvation. Center your heart and mind on the grace He has given us.

If you haven't trusted Jesus nor responded by faith to the forgiveness He offers, God has a gift for you today. Simply ask.

Reflect With God

Consider the truth of Matthew 1:21, and respond to this teaching with prayer.

"I waited patiently for the Lord; he inclined to me and heard my cry. He drew me up from the pit of destruction... and set my feet upon a rock, making my steps secure. He put a new song in my mouth, a song of praise to our God..." (Psalm 40:1-3)

God's Promise for Today - *Matthew 2:11*

"And going into the house, they saw the child with Mary his mother, and they fell down and worshiped him. Then, opening their treasures, they offered him gifts, gold and frankincense and myrrh."

Consider Today's Truth

Consumers Like Us

This is the season when we are bombarded with ads for "the perfect Christmas gift." Trinkets and tools. Shirts and socks. Devices and diamonds. Christmas is time to sell anything and everything. Many jump into the swing of things. They buy what they do not need to give to people they may not know, spending money they do not have! Our consumeristic bend is stoked at Christmas. We tend to go overboard. We compete with the price tag. We measure love by the number of presents we receive. If someone asks why we give presents at Christmas, they are directed to the Magi as our example.

The Magi

Magi refers to a group of astrologers from the east. The Bible speaks of them as wise men, proficient in studying and interpreting the sky. They observed an unusual star, which led them to search for a child born King of the Jews. This group of an unknown number went to Jerusalem and were directed to Bethlehem by biblical prophecy. King Herod heard this as a threat and directed them to let him know where the child was. His intent was wicked. The Magi traveled from Jerusalem to Bethlehem, led by the star and found the house of Joseph, Mary and Jesus. With joy, they entered and fell prostrate in worship. They offered expensive and precious gifts. God warned them in a dream not to return to Herod.

If we want to use their example as a motive for gift giving to one another, we miss the point. Their gifts were an expression of worship to God, not mutual love and appreciation for one another. They offered their treasure in adoration for Jesus the King. If their example teaches us anything, it's this: Christmas is not for our personal consumption. Christmas is a time to worship Jesus.

Jesus Is the Reason

The central theme of Matthew's gospel is that Jesus is the King. He is the rightful heir to David's throne. He is the one to rule over everything. To emphasize his point, Matthew highlights the Magi. These were Gentiles looking for the King of the Jews and worshiping Jesus. Jesus is Lord, not only of Jews, but of all people.

If we are going to approach Christmas with a biblical foundation, our focus will be on the worship of Jesus Christ. Our culture has shaped Christmas as a time for children. Wide-eyed toddlers searching the sky for Santa's sleigh. We enlarge our celebration to include opportunity for family traditions, visits and feasts. We may even go so far as to think of Christmas as a period of peace and good will to all. We smile at strangers and are cordial to cashiers. "If we do all of this, certainly we are fulfilling the meaning of Christmas!"

We do Christmas right when we keep Jesus as central. The layers we have added may be delightful and helpful, but they are non-essentials. Worship is the essential to the season.

Receive God's Promise

Worship is not only essential, but also remedial. Worship keeps our heads and hearts ordered aright. The antidote to consumerism is a worshipful realignment that Christmas is not about us. Worship doesn't diminish our delight. It fills our hearts with joy over the grace and mercy of our God. And it is a joy which lasts. A worshipping heart can experience Christmas all year round.

Reflect With God

Consider the truth of Matthew 2:11, and respond to this teaching with prayer.

"God is our refuge and strength, a very present help in trouble. Therefore we will not fear though the earth gives way, though the mountains be moved into the heart of the sea." (Psalm 46:1-2)

God's Promise for Today - *Matthew 2:18*

"A voice was heard in Ramah, weeping and loud lamentation, Rachel weeping for her children; she refused to be comforted, because they are no more."

Consider Today's Truth

Not Immune

The day after Christmas in 2004, Thailand experienced the deadliest tsunami ever recorded. Over 230,000 people were killed. It was a devastation difficult to absorb, made even more stunning by its timing.

We tend to think of Christmas as if it were Disneyland. Everything is bright, happy, and delightful. There may be crime or poverty outside the perimeter of Disneyland, but nothing bad happens inside the Magic Kingdom. It jars us to think that Christmas is not immune to the pains and problems of life. Heart attacks. Hunger. Angry words. Car accidents. Violence. Death. It can all happen at Christmas. It happened at the first Christmas.

Weeping

Herod was a ruthless man. History records his violence against his own family. It was not a stretch for him to entertain violence against others - especially if he perceived a threat to his throne. The Magi alerted Herod to news of a new king. Herod was uncertain about the timing, but he had the location. His scribes and priests pointed to Bethlehem. Enraged that he had been duped by the Magi, Herod ordered that all the male children 2 and under were to be killed in Bethlehem and the surrounding vicinity. Pause on that. Consider the fear, the panicked attempts to escape and the painful wailing of parents. We don't know how many children were slaughtered, but the number is not the issue. There is enough pain in one heart to last a lifetime.

Deaf to the Carols

Christmas is not without pain. It is presented as a time for joy, but not all feel it. The homeless on our streets do not think of trees and gifts. Refugees fleeing gunfire don't give thought to decorations. A widow sitting at a table with an empty chair isn't concerned about the menu. This tends to be the season with the most anxiety, tension, loneliness, and depression. The happy songs in the mall must sound like a mockery to some.

If these words sound out of sync and you don't want to think about it lest they ruin your Christmas, read the first Christmas again. Christmas doesn't banish the dark. God steps into our world with all its darkness and brings mercy and compassion. He doesn't promise there will be no hurt. He does promise to be Immanuel.

Receive God's Promise

Accepting that difficulty is not strange to the season frees us in two ways. Firstly, we can drop all pretense. We want to project smiles and abundance, but that may not be how we feel or what we have. We present a facade to all around us and keep it up before God. But our tears and troubles find mercy and help. Jesus came to our world and lived our life. He can give us grace in the time of our need (Hebrews 4:16).

Secondly, we can recognize the needs in others. By admitting that Christmas is not exempt from struggles, our eyes are open to those experiencing hardship around us. The mercy we receive becomes mercy we can give.

Reflect With God

Consider the truth of Matthew 2:18, and respond to this teaching with prayer.

WEEK 4 *Love - We Give Him Our Heart*

We Give Him Our Heart

Hope, peace, joy and now the Advent weeks turn to love. It's not hard to make the connection between Christmas and love. Every gift and gesture offered to those around you is an expression of your heart. Christmas is the announcement that "God so loved that He gave." It is also an opportunity for us to offer Him our hearts of gratitude, devotion and praise.

Mary is an example of love for God. This week, the focus will be on her response to the miracle of God's plan. We can catch glimpses of how we, too, can express our love for our Lord.

You are invited to spend time in the series, *The Word Became Flesh*, a Christmas perspective from the Apostle John, found on the Back to the Bible Canada website, **backtothebible.ca**

God's Promise for Today - *Luke 1:28-29*

"And he came to her and said, 'Greetings, O favoured one, the Lord is with you!' But she was greatly troubled at the saying, and tried to discern what sort of greeting this might be."

Consider Today's Truth

We Blush

It is common for many to deflect a compliment. Some duck and dodge when skills or achievements are applauded. It might be out of a sense of humility as a guardrail against falling into pride. It could be from a deeper source. Since we know ourselves better than anyone else knows us, our imperfections and failures are obvious. These become the filter through which we receive kindness, appreciation or even love. Our blemishes convince us that the favour extended to us is misplaced. So, we diminish them.

Gabriel's Message

Gabriel was dispatched to a teenage girl in Nazareth. Mary was betrothed to Joseph, anticipating the type of life she saw other young women experiencing in her small town. Everything was about to change through an angelic visitation. Gabriel's first words stated that Mary had favour with God and that God was with her. This troubled Mary. She couldn't understand what type of greeting this was. Whatever fear Mary felt would be understandable, but even this was addressed by Gabriel with the same message, "You have found favour with God!"

Even before the message of a virgin birth was spoken, Mary

struggled to accept the words. She couldn't process them. "What did I ever do to gain the favour of God? Why would God see and care about me?" She had no status in society. She had done nothing noteworthy before men or God. While her spiritual life was devout, it didn't reach the level of heavenly gossip. Mary had difficulty believing that God would mark her for special favour. We do the same.

Struggle With Grace

Grace is the message that God has put His favour upon us regardless of our performance, quality or worth. Grace is the smile of God, untied to any reason we can come up with to explain it. So it is a hard message for us to embrace. If God were to chide us, we would understand. If God dispensed punishment for our offence, we would agree we had it coming. If God did not speak or tend to us, we would conclude that He was busy running the universe. We want His voice and need His help, but we can see abundant cause for our disqualification.

Grace is a hard message to accept. We don't witness this grace in our world. We understand cause and effect, crime and punishment, reward and penalty. But to be loved without condition, welcomed despite repeated failures and embraced even when we were enemies, this can only be from God.

Understand, God is no "softy." He is not a grandfather who overlooks our faults and is convinced we can do no wrong. Grace flows because of Jesus Christ. He came into this world that He might show us who God is (John 1:14). He came to pay the penalty for our wrongs - for every sin, for all eternity (2 Corinthians 5:21). That is the message of God's grace.

Receive God's Promise

We believe this message by faith and live by that same faith. Grace is so radical that we must keep returning to it. We return to the unmerited love of God, not to brace it up, but that we might be braced by its truth. When you find yourself guilty of a repeated sin, God has grace for you. When you are overwhelmed by a sense of inadequacy, there is grace for you. When you feel distant and dry of soul, Christ's favour remains. Today and all the tomorrows to come, receive His grace.

Reflect With God

Consider the truth of Luke 1:28-29, and respond to this teaching with prayer.

A Great Responsibility

Collect Yourself Before God

"Hear my cry, O God, listen to my prayer; from the end of the earth I call to you when my heart is faint. Lead me to the rock that is higher than I, for you have been my refuge, a strong tower against the enemy." (Psalm 61:1-3)

God's Promise for Today - Luke 1:32-33

"He will be great and will be called the Son of the Most High. And the Lord will give to him the throne of his father David, and he will reign over the house of Jacob forever, and of his kingdom there will be no end."

Consider Today's Truth

Stewards of Life

Every first-time parent feels a huge responsibility as they take their newborn home. This is all new and they aren't sure if they can do it. How will they know what the child needs? How long should they let them cry? What if they get sick? Eventually, parents understand that there is more to raising a child than keeping them fed and safe. They want to prepare them for life. Music lessons, choosing a school, sports teams, manners, chores, choosing friends - all these skills are to be modeled and instilled. After all, their child may become a doctor, teacher, lawyer or civic leader. We want to prepare our children for what they will be. What if the child was to be a King?

A King in the Nursery

Mary was overwhelmed by Gabriel's pronouncement of God's grace. But the angelic message became even heavier. Her child Jesus had a magnificent future. He would be known as the Son of God. He would grow to be the ruler of Israel, and His Kingdom would be unceasing. How could Mary raise such a great King? What could she teach Him about ruling? How could she prepare Him for the role God had for Him? What if she made a mistake?

We have little in the Scriptures

about Jesus' household experience. We can assume that Mary and Joseph told Jesus the details of His birth - Gabriel's message, angels, shepherds and Magi. Joseph taught carpentry to Jesus. We know they took Him to the temple and must have provided a grounding in the Scriptures. Beyond that, there is nothing in the home we know of that catered to Jesus' future reign. The most significant training that Mary and Joseph could offer was love.

Of course, the education and shaping of Jesus was not simply up to Mary and Joseph. God was at work. God would make Jesus King.

The Spirit was upon Jesus, shaping Him in obedience and maturity. The Father would declare from the heavens, "This is my beloved Son, with whom I am well pleased" (Matthew 3:17). Mary and Joseph did what they ought to do, but the Hand of God was active, doing only what He could do.

Not Just Us Working

It's an important lesson for us all. For our children, jobs, houses, finances and relationships. We have responsibility for each, but God is at work. The mistakes we make need not be disastrous. The success we have may not be determinative. Our lives are not simply the product of our hands, but the blessing of God in and through the work of our hands (Psalm 90:17).

No Christian parent raises their child alone. No Christian grandparent need feel helpless as they watch the coming generations. God is at work. He is active in family, occupations, neighbourhoods, governments, schools, and congregations. We have a stewardship to fulfill with the people, gifting and opportunity God sends us. God does not simply watch us, but works in and through us.

Receive God's Promise

Where in your life do you sense vulnerability? Your children, grandchildren, parents or spouse? You are not sure that they will be all that God intends. You are not sure you have done everything possible. But remember, even when you have done all that you could, God is doing more.

Reflect With God

Consider the truth of Luke 1:32-33, and respond to this teaching with prayer.

Collect Yourself Before God

"For God alone, O my soul, wait in silence, for my hope is from him. He only is my rock and my salvation, my fortress; I shall not be shaken... Trust in him at all times, O people; pour out your heart before him; God is a refuge for us." (Psalm 62:5-6,8)

God's Promise for Today - *Luke 1:38*

"And Mary said, 'Behold, I am the servant of the Lord, let it be to me according to your word.' And the angel departed from her."

Consider Today's Truth

Courageous Acts

What's the most courageous thing you have ever done? For some it's bungee jumping. For others it may be moving to another country or facing cancer treatment. Courage has many faces. There is physical courage, courage of convictions, financial audacity or boldness in relationships. Faith is its own kind of courage. Mary, young as she was, had it to the full measure.

I Am Your Servant

Gabriel's visit was an overload of information, about Mary and about the child that would be born.

It must have seemed too much to take in. But the hardest part was yet to come. Gabriel said that she would have a child. Mary knew that she couldn't. She was not married and had never been unfaithful. Virgins do not give birth. She asked, "How will this be?" Her question had two concerns: How can this be, physically? How can this be proper or moral? Gabriel's answer to both questions was the same. The Holy Spirit would overshadow Mary so she would conceive, and the child born would be holy - the Son of God. The angel gave Mary assurance that what had never happened before in history would take place. Mary's relative Elizabeth was thought to be barren, but was now in her 6th month of pregnancy, "For nothing will be impossible with God."

Mary's leap of faith was large. The pain of small-town gossip was inevitable. Damage to her relationship with Joseph was likely. The risk of family rejection, bearing a stained reputation and being ridiculed as crazy for her explanation – none of this was out of the question. But Mary said "Yes." She didn't have to, but she agreed to God's plan. She saw herself as a servant of God and submitted to His will.

Love Says Yes

Often, the vows in a wedding ceremony contain the promise of, "I will. I do." The covenant of matrimony begins with a "yes." For better or worse, yes! Richer or poorer, yes! In sickness and health, yes! As time unfolds, there will be situations that press against that initial willingness. The vows will be tested. Here is a secret: the more we love, the more we say "yes." And the more we say, "yes," the more we will love.

What is true in the covenantal relationship of marriage is true of our covenant with God. We said "yes" to God in our first expression of faith. Throughout our pilgrimage, we learn to repeat our "yes" to Him. Jesus said that if we love Him, we will keep His commandments (John 14:15). At times, our affirmation of His command is given grudgingly. We respond more out of duty than devotion. Yet the more we obey, the more devotion will grow. Our "yes" turns into love.

Receive God's Promise

Is there a place where you are saying "no" to God? It may not be outright rebellion, maybe just avoidance or delay. We find different ways of ducking obedience while convincing ourselves that we're innocent of defiance. If we know God is speaking to us and we resist compliance, our hearts grow stale. It is better to see ourselves as God's servants. Be it unto us according to your word. The root of obedient duty blossoms into the devotion of love.

Reflect With God

Consider the truth of Luke 1:38, and respond to this teaching with prayer.

God's Promise for Today - *Luke 1:46-49*

"And Mary said, 'My soul magnifies the Lord, and my spirit rejoices in God my Savior, for he has looked on the humble estate of his servant. For behold, from now on all generations will call me blessed; for he who is mighty has done great things for me, and holy is his name.'"

Consider Today's Truth

Gone too Far?

We have become accustomed to products that have warning labels. In food packaging, with electronic devices or vehicles, there are warnings that caution us about misuse. Some of them seem odd, even humorous. For a hair dryer, "Never use while sleeping." For a power drill, "Not intended for use as a dental drill." For birthday candles, "Do not use soft wax as ear plugs." Clearly, the labels are to avoid litigation in case of mishap, but the cautions seem extreme when compared to the reality. In some churches, Christmas arrives with an assumed warning label, "Don't talk too much about Mary!"

One can't help but read through the first two chapters of Luke and not think of Mary. As a follower of Jesus, she has a very significant place of honour and importance in the story of faith.

Too Much or Too Little?

When it comes to an understanding of Mary, there are clearly errors to avoid. It is possible to elevate Mary to a role and status that belongs only to God. So, to ensure that we don't make too much of Mary, we can become guilty of making too little of her as well.

Mary's place in Scripture and history is unique. No one else has ever been graced to be the mother of Jesus. She was given the privilege of bearing the Son of God, and then, together with Joseph, to nurture, teach and train Him from His youth. Her assignment was great, and her faith was great as well. Her submission to the will of God and trust to embrace His work is a model for all believers. The New Testament record of Mary demonstrates her faithfulness, from the announcement of her conception of Jesus, to the coming of the Spirit at Pentecost (Acts 1:14). We can learn from Mary.

God Has Done Great Things for Me

When Mary met with Elizabeth, these two women shared the joy and praise of being graced by God. Elizabeth speaks a blessing to Mary because she believed the promise of the Lord. In response, Mary bursts into praise. It is a song called the Magnificat (Luke 1:46-55). Her first words were, "My soul magnifies the Lord." God cannot be made larger, but within her own soul, Mary proclaims that she is enlarging God. She is making room for God to occupy the fullness of her spirit. She is God-focused. Within her soul, she celebrates who God is. She is humbled by what God has promised and concludes that God has done great things for her!

That is a needed Christmas perspective. Through the festivities of the season, we want to magnify God in our hearts. We want to be God-focused. There are so many details, activities, obligations, and intentions that compete for space and time in our hearts and minds. We may feel like God is being squeezed out! Mary is centered on God, filled with joy by His presence and humbled by His goodness. She shows us how to celebrate Christmas.

Receive God's Promise

The push and pull for our attention reaches a climax every Christmas. We want to be attentive to God first, but family, church and community all demand space in our heads and hearts. It can be too much. How can we follow the example of Mary? We can note the ways God has been good to us. We can carve priority space in our day to speak with God. We can view the details of our lives as avenues of God's activity. We can magnify the Lord together in worship. It will be a Christmas celebration that honours God.

Reflect With God

Consider the truth of Luke 1:46-49, and respond to this teaching with prayer.

Collect Yourself Before God

"May God be gracious to us and bless us and make his face to shine upon us, that your way may be known on earth, your saving power among all nations." (Psalm 67:1-2)

God's Promise for Today - *Luke 2:7*

"And she gave birth to her firstborn son and wrapped him in swaddling clothes and laid him in a manger, because there was no place for them in the inn."

Consider Today's Truth

Beginnings

Most beginnings are small. The world's richest company started in a garage with two employees. Giant cedars begin as tiny seeds. The Fraser River moves 1,375 km but starts as a dripping spring in the Rockies. We all arrive in this world weighing little and knowing less. Our arrival is cause for celebration, but within a small circle of relatives and friends. Most of the world didn't even know that you showed up.

Jesus Arrives

The arrival of God into our world went unnoticed. The talk of the town was about political decisions. A census was decreed, and lives got disrupted. Since Joseph was from Bethlehem, he had to be registered there. It was an onerous four-day journey for anyone, more so for a pregnant woman. Bethlehem was bustling with activity, so no one noticed when a young woman delivered her first born and laid Him in a feeding trough. The Messiah had come, but the world spun as normal.

God could not let His Son arrive without celebration. A host of angels were sent to shepherds outside of Bethlehem. They announced good news of great joy about a Saviour born! The shepherds ran to find Mary, Joseph and the baby. They reported to His parents all that the angels said of the child. Then the shepherds left, and all was still. Heaven was loud with praise, but Bethlehem was silent with the sounds of the night.

The Day of Small Things

The arrival of Jesus went largely overlooked. God arrived in a small town that struggled to host Him. His coming was humbly subtle. It seems to be the way of God. He leaves the pomp and ceremony for those who seem to need it. God comes in a burning bush, a whispered voice, a manger. He can throw lightning bolts and shake the ground with His presence, but He prefers to arrive in hidden ways to unremarkable people. That doesn't mean that His purpose and intent are small - they are not! Yet His eternal, vast plans have modest beginnings.

Jesus chose a dozen men to unfold a great Kingdom. His Spirit fell to just 120 in an upper room and flowed through Jerusalem, Judea, Samaria and the remote parts of this world. We are cautioned not to misinterpret small beginnings (Zechariah 4:10). It is the wisdom of God to start small. Small beginnings allow time to grow and to grow strong and deep. They require patience, a fruit that God grows in us. They testify to the presence and power of God. No one else can make something so great from something so small. Creation begins with a word. God comes as a baby. Eternal life begins with a "yes" to Jesus.

Receive God's Promise

Review the things that seem small in your life - too small to be of any great effect. If God can feed a crowd with 5 loaves and 2 fish, could He utilize what seems meager to you? We often wait until we can offer God something great; large numbers, serious capacity, significant vision. But if God often begins with the small things in hidden places, give that to Him now. Watch what He will do with your obedience.

Reflect With God

Consider the truth of Luke 2:7, and respond to this teaching with prayer.

Collect Yourself Before God

"May all who seek you rejoice and be glad in you! May those who love your salvation say evermore, 'God is great!' But I am poor and needy; hasten to me, O God! You are my help and my deliverer; O Lord, do not delay!" (Psalm 70:4-5)

God's Promise for Today - *Luke 2:34-35*

"And Simeon blessed them and said to Mary his mother, 'Behold, this child is appointed for the fall and rising of many in Israel, and for a sign that is opposed (and a sword will pierce through your own soul also), so that thoughts from many hearts may be revealed.'"

Consider Today's Truth

Love Has a Price

Love is not painless. It carries with it the likelihood of being wounded. Every relationship has the possibility of hurt. You can love and not be loved back. The ones you love may not always be loveable. Words can be said without thought, regrettable actions that can't be undone, distance and silence hard to bear. There is a way to avoid all these pains. Don't give your heart to anyone; but if you do love, know there is a price to pay.

Jesus Misunderstood and Rejected

Simeon was a righteous man looking for the Messiah. Simeon held on to God's promise that he would see the Lord's anointed in his lifetime. When Mary and Joseph brought the infant Jesus into the temple, Simeon knew He was the One. Simeon blessed the parents and then spoke directly to Mary. This child would elevate some, but trip up others. Jesus would reveal the hearts of men. Not everyone would applaud the child. Not everyone would receive the child. Jesus would be misunderstood. Jesus came to His own and was rejected (John 1:11). He would pay a price for His love. In fact, Mary would bear her own portion of pain for the love she had for her child. A sword would pierce her heart. Her Son would be crucified.

God Pays a Price for Love

God is not immune to the price of love. He too cannot love without the possibility of being hurt. And He is hurt. He grieves over the hardness of His people throughout the Old Testament (Psalm 81:13). Jesus laments over Jerusalem (Matthew 23:37). The Spirit of God can be grieved (Ephesians 4:30). God created us and loves us, yet throughout history, God is maligned, misunderstood, ignored, criticized and mocked. Still, He continues to shower the earth with grace. He extends favour to each person in countless ways. He is patient and persistent with His love. He does not stop loving when the price is high. He loves the world and sent His only Son to die for us.

As children of God and followers of Jesus, we can expect to share in the cost of love. We are not immune to the heartache of rejection, persecution, misunderstanding or distance. In fact, it may come from our own family, those we deeply love. When we suffer for Christ's sake, if our biblical values are not embraced, our faith is not practiced by family or friends, we will feel the ache. In those moments, remember that we are sharing the pain God feels. God understands what it is to love and not be loved in return. When we share in the heartbreak of God, remember He knows how we feel.

Receive God's Promise

Do you have loved ones for whom your heart breaks for Jesus' sake? Have you been hurt by those you love because of your faith in Jesus? When our love for Jesus and our love for others do not harmonize, we feel tension and grief. The resolution to that struggle is not to love them or Jesus any less, but to bring our wounded heart before the God who understands. He feels the same wounds.

Reflect With God

Consider the truth of Luke 2:34-35, and respond to this teaching with prayer.

Collect Yourself Before God

"Incline Your ear, O Lord, and answer me, for I am poor and needy. Preserve my life, for I am godly; save your servant, who trusts in you—you are my God...For you, O Lord, are good and forgiving, abounding in steadfast love to all who call upon you." (Psalm 86:1-2,5)

God's Promise for Today - *Luke 2:49-50*

"And he said to them, 'Why were you looking for me? Did you not know that I must be in my Father's house?' And they did not understand the saying that he spoke to them."

Consider Today's Truth

Repeated but Not Exhausted

We do this every year. Annually, we anticipate and celebrate Christmas. We often do the same things every year. We pull out the same lights we did last year and use decorations for the tree that have a long history with us. In church, we sing carols that we learned as a child. We read the Scriptures about angels, shepherds, Magi and a manger. How can we repeat our traditions without being stale? How can we tell the same story over and over? We can because Christmas is a truth that is not exhausted. There is much we can learn over a lifetime.

Mary Didn't Understand

Luke includes an anecdote of Jesus, unrecorded in other gospels. Joseph and Mary went annually to Jerusalem for the Passover. When Jesus was 12 years old, they went as usual. On their return journey, they lost track of Jesus among relatives and friends. It took three days of frantic searching until they found Him back in Jerusalem in the temple. You can imagine their emotional state. When Mary asked, "How could you treat us this way?" she didn't understand

Jesus' reply. "Didn't you know I must be in my Father's house?" The parents didn't understand.

There was plenty of evidence to suggest that Jesus was different from all others. Gabriel's message. The shepherd's account of angels. Magi come to worship. Simeon and Anna's prophetic words. The parents knew all of this, but there was much they still had to learn about Jesus. It is evident in the gospels that both Mary and her other children struggled to grasp Jesus' intent and purpose (Mark 3:21; Matthew 12:48). It was only after the resurrection that some of Jesus' brothers came to believe in Him. So, it is possible to be with Jesus up close and still not see the full picture.

The Depth of Christmas

Christmas is a treasure of truth in which mysteries and wonders are held. It is a story of God who keeps His covenant. It is the account of creation's redemption begun on earth. It teaches of a virgin birth giving life to the holy Son of God. Christmas is a mystery of the God/Man –Jesus, who is fully human and fully God, both at once. We read the narrative of God who grows, "strong, filled with wisdom. And the favor of God was upon him" (Luke 2:40). Christmas displays the power of God to do the impossible for the need of mankind which is humanly insurmountable. This is a story of love and grace. Love stories do not grow old. It is possible for us to celebrate Christmas repeatedly because we have so much to learn. We know the details of the story, but we are learning of Jesus.

Receive God's Promise

What is your favourite part of the Christmas story? Is there a part that you love to hear even though you have heard it before? What have you learned of Christmas that impacts your soul? We will avoid boredom or being bound by our customs as we continually focus on Jesus. We do not worship a story, but our Lord.

Reflect With God

Consider the truth of Luke 2:49-50, and respond to this teaching with prayer.

Week 4: Love
Heart Treasure

"He who dwells in the shelter of the Most High will abide in the shadow of the Almighty. I will say to the Lord, 'My refuge and my fortress, my God, in whom I trust." (Psalm 91:1-2)

God's Promise for Today - *Luke 2:19, 51*

"But Mary treasured up all these things, pondering them in her heart.... And he went down with them and came to Nazareth and was submissive to them. And his mother treasured up all these things in her heart."

Consider Today's Truth

Souvenirs

Some people have spoon collections as mementos of visited destinations. Each spoon dishes a different memory. We take infinite photos of our children and store them as stories to be retold throughout the years. We buy souvenirs at gift shops to take our holidays home with us. Souvenir is French for "remember," and that is what these trinkets do for us. They help us recall the times, places, events, and people that have enriched our living.

Mary Remembered

Twice Luke records that Mary had a place in her heart for memories. When the shepherds left to return to their fields, Mary treasured what they said in her heart. When Jesus was apparently lost and then found doing what He said He must be doing, Mary stored that as a treasured memory as well. Every parent holds on to the significant stages of a child's growth. Yet it is telling that what Mary stored was not about Jesus' first words or steps. Luke writes that she held on to the things that reminded her Jesus was unique. Angelic voices and temple visits. Because it wasn't just memories she was holding. She reflected upon what they meant.

Luke says Mary pondered them in her heart. This was not

an exercise of recall, but a desire to understand. Mary wanted to know what these events meant. What was God doing? How should she understand Jesus her son? She considered these memories over and over. Mary probably had many more to ponder. Candlelight conversations with Jesus. Questions He would ask her. Watching Him recite His prayers. Listening to Him interact with His friends. Hearing Him speak of His sense of mission as He put down His carpentry tools. Mary had much to ponder.

Truth in Our Hearts

Pondering is an exercise of both the mind and heart. Pondering suggests that our reflective thought isn't easily finished. We don't necessarily have clear-cut answers. We must mull over the mystery that's before us.

Pondering isn't about discovering answers, but insight. That's why it is a heart exercise as well. We must be patient and remain engaged, even if insight takes a while. We will have to be content with partial knowing or even unknowing. A wise father tells his son to listen to his words and keep them in his heart (Proverbs 4:20-21). That is what pondering does.

Christmas is an opportunity to hold the treasures of Immanuel and consider their importance and meaning. It is a rational thing, to read and study. It is a heartfelt thing, to pray and reflect. The truths will enrich our mind and soul. We will find answers and even more questions. We will be struck with wonder and awe over our God.

Mary considered the mysteries of her Son to be worth holding on to and pondering about. We should too.

Receive God's Promise

What part of the Christmas truth piques your curiosity? What part stirs your heart? How will you not pack Christmas away on December 31st, but treasure the truth in your heart?

Reflect With God

Consider the truth of Luke 2:19, 51, and respond to this teaching with prayer.

Collect Yourself Before God

"Satisfy us in the morning with your steadfast love, that we may rejoice and be glad all our days...Let the favor of the Lord our God be upon us, and establish the work of our hands upon us; yes, establish the work of our hands!" (Psalm 90:14,17)

God's Promise for Today - *John 1:14, 16-18*

"And the Word became flesh and dwelt among us, and we have seen his glory, glory as of the only Son from the Father, full of grace and truth....for from his fullness we have all received, grace upon grace. For the Law was given through Moses; grace and truth came through Jesus Christ. No one has ever seen God; the only God, who is at the Father's side, he has made him known."

Consider Today's Truth

Grace Comes Like Waves From an Ocean

John says that each one of us has been graced by Jesus. We have all received grace upon grace. We have spent four weeks thinking from the biblical account of God's grace at Christmas - Hope, Peace, Joy and Love. The people of the Scriptures, Isaiah, Zechariah, Joseph and Mary, have turned our attention to God's ultimate grace – Jesus Christ, His Son.

It's safe to assume that the stories mentioned were not new to you. You have heard the details of Christmas before. But life demands more than one breath. We breathe repeatedly. One meal can't sustain. We eat daily. We don't turn to Christmas because it is novel, but because it is necessary. It is a story of God's life, light and love among us. It promises that same life, light and love for us - even today. Our Christmas celebration is done, but our worship of the Son given never ends.

Reflections

Families may have a habit of gathering their Christmas gifts under the tree once they have been opened. It allows all to take note of the kindness that's been given. Take some time to review any reflections, insights, or observations you have made in the last 30 days.

- What grace has God granted you in your reading, thoughts and prayers?

- Did you discover something about Christmas? What was it?

- How have the expectations you wrote on Day 1 unfolded?

- Which Advent grace is most needed for you right now - Hope? Peace? Joy? Love?

Reflect With God

Consider the truth of John 1:14, 16-18, and respond to this teaching with prayer.

"But grow in the grace and knowledge of our Lord and Savior Jesus Christ. To him be the glory both now and to the day of eternity. Amen."
2 Peter 3:18

NOTES

www.ingramcontent.com/pod-product-compliance
Lightning Source LLC
Chambersburg PA
CBHW051332120626
46547CB00016B/2511